The Power of Expectations: To Get What You Want You Must Expect It to Happen

Category: Business & Economics

Author: Bob Oros

Publisher: Bob Oros Publishing

ISBN: 978-1-387-19891-7

Copyright 2017

I0475694

Description: Make the call expecting people to see you. Expect them to treat you with respect. Expect them to listen to you. Expect them to answer your questions. Expect them to buy. Expecting things to happen will have a huge impact on the results. Once you master this skill you will never feel insecure or worried about business.

Key words: sales coaching, sales techniques, motivating sales people, job in sales, sales manager training, sales course, manufacturing sales training, wholesale sales training, online sales training, distributor sales training, food sales jobs, food service sales,

ISBN 978-1-387-19891-7

9 781387 198917

THE POWER OF EXPECTATIONS: TO GET WHAT YOU WANT YOU MUST EXPECT IT TO HAPPEN

1. What do your expectations have to do with selling?

Do you go into each sales call with the HOPE of making a sale, but not necessarily expecting it so you won't be disappointed?

In a recent test researchers found out that if they put a blindfold over someone while they are eating, they eat less. Let's take this another step and ask ourselves this; what if all of a sudden you or I lost our memory and our sight at the same time? What if no one would tell us how old we were and we would have to guess?

What would you say?

Now let's take it another step and ask ourselves what if we were unable to remember any of our past failures and disappointments, but could only remember our successes. What if someone followed us around all week with a movie camera and edited out all the stupid stuff we did? At the end of the week they played everything we did right, every success regardless of how small it was and removed all the bloopers.

Now let's go one step further. Let's say that you are a researcher rather than a sales person. Your job is to do market research and find out why people buy or don't buy. Your success is not going to be determined by whether you make a sale on that particular call, but your success is going to be determined by doing the research.

You make the call expecting people to see you. You expect them to treat you with respect. You expect them to listen to you. You expect them to answer your questions. If the timing is right and what you are offering is the solution to their problem, you expect them to buy. If the timing is not right, or the solution is not a good fit, you would expect them not to buy.

At the end of the day when someone asked you how your day went, how would you answer? Would you say you were a success or a failure? No. You would say I talked to 15 people. Two of them were having problems and I was able to offer a solution. Ten of them were happy with what they were doing but agreed to have me come back at a specific time in the near future. Three of them had very closed minds and were not open to anything new regardless of how bad they needed it.

So instead of making the call as a typical sales person, make the call like a consultant would.

For example: "I am doing some research in the area to find out if our services would be beneficial. Do you mind if I ask you three questions and it will only take three minutes to answer?"

So, if we put a blindfold on you that filtered out the normal fear a person has when approaching a stranger while trying to sell them something, what's left? Confident expectations of doing the job. And the action will create hope, which comes from doing the details of the job exceptionally well. And when you do your job exceptionally well, it is impossible to be disappointed.

Knowing exactly what you want, expecting to get it and visualizing the outcome is effectively managing your attitude. When you spend time planning your strategies you are creating a situation you desire. You have control over the outcome.

If you are not advancing towards your goal with the expectation of success, it is not the goal that is out of reach. It is the daily activities that need attention. The common denominator of all successful professional people is the same. THEY ALL EXPECT TO SUCCEED.

The common denominator of all unsuccessful sales people is the same. Deep down inside – THEY ALL EXPECT TO FAIL.

Look at a successful surgeon. When they operate on someone they have the positive expectation of success.

A lawyer is another good example. When they are addressing the jury they have the 100% positive expectation of convincing the jury to see things from his or her point of view.

A politician must have the expectation of success. If you interview several candidates running for the same office the night before election, they would all believe they won. If they lost this expectation of winning at any point during the campaign they would immediately be out of the race.

However, there is a difference.

Most professional people must go through several years of higher education before actually starting in their profession. All during these years the attitude of high expectations is slowly building day by day. Once they have invested in four, six or eight years of education they feel they have earned the right to expect success. And they have.

Compare that to the profession of sales. If you have never sold a thing in your life, have very little formal education and are looking for a job – you can start a career in sales tomorrow! The profession will welcome you with open arms no matter what your background, experience or education may or may not be.

In sales you have not had the day-by-day, year-by-year preparation that most professions have. You may go through a short company training program that pumps up your expectations to a high level, however, once you enter the real world, alone and unprepared for what's next, your expectations take a downward turn and things look different.

To succeed there has to be certain things in harmony. Your expectations and your goals must be equal. If your goals are too high or unrealistic you won't expect to reach them and you will see to it that you get what you expect.

Your goals must be clearly defined, realistic, reachable and most importantly APPROACHED WITH THE POSITIVE EXPECTATION OF SUCCESS.

Without the advantage of having four years of sales training before making your first sales call, you have to take a different approach. You have to teach yourself this important principle of selling – to expect success.

Good idea. Rather than remembering (and dreading) how disappointing cold calling can be, as an established rep with a successful route I might better focus on the success stories with my current accounts rather than worry about being rejected by a potential new account. Focusing on just how much I do and how well I perform with my top accounts will give me the proper attitude to approach prospective new business. THEY know I'm good and if I remember that and embrace it, it will show to the person I am approaching and be plainly evident that I am someone they NEED to help their business.

Chris Chase

This could be the closest thing to the silver bullet. Over the years as I watched and learned from successful associates, many times I could not see any discernable evidence of exceptional skill or talent, yet they were so successful. These people always seemed so at ease and so very confident. THEY EXPECTED to win!

Doug Barringer

I listened to an insperational recording with the name of "Pigs don't know pigs stink."

My interpretation of this is if I don't know I can't succeed then I believe I will succeed. If I don't know I can't fail then I believe I can't fail.   Use your mistakes to improve yourself. My supervisor has told me that if you learn from a mistake nothing was lost. If you keep making the same mistake over and over we have a problem.

Ralph Scalici

This article was inspiring. Every one wants to succeed, not only in sales but in life itself. It takes a lot of hard work, planning, dedication, and realistic expectations. Being a single mother for the last 12 years I understand what it's like to want to be successful. After being out of school for over 13 years I new that the only way I was going to be successful in raising my two children I would have to return to school so that I could get a better job making more than minimum wage. I've come along way since then. I now have two grown children and one grandson. Staying positive even when things got ruff helped my children and I get to this point in our life's as well as our working lives. There are still things I want to accomplish before I'm done, so I will approach each one of my goals one at the time. But keeping positive, motivated and working hard daily to achieve them one day at the time.

Laura Arnett

I feel expecting success is a huge part of being successful. However, each small success can put you in the right frame of mind. I try to remember the FIRST time I made a sale and how great it felt. This often times carries me through the rough spots.

Tonya Sauer

This is very true. When I started out selling I had a bad habit of putting my goals way to high and my expectations were much to low. It was a frame of mind that I had to get myself out of because I knew I would not succeed like that. I made my goals and expectations match which in time turned into a successful relationship. After that I would expect to reach my goals because they were within my reach.

Brandon Sanchez

This is so true, in most professions there are years of training, education etc... When starting in sales with the lack of training & education, it is important to make realistic expectations or you will only set yourself up for failure. With clear defined goals that are achievable, then a sales person will have the correct mind from the beginning & will be able to complete their goals & be successful. A person starting off with a mind set geared towards knowing they won't be able to accomplish the goal will only hinder them from giving their 110% and they will convenience themselves into "why try" to accomplish something that is unreachable. Having a positive attitude and strong confidence in your ability to succeed will make the difference in whether they will become a successful sales person or just mediocre.

Carla McCrea

Expectations: If you don't BELIEVE you can do it – you never will. Can a man run a mile in under four minutes? Fact: the 4-minute mile was once thought to be physically impossible by informed observers. Many tried and failed; deep inside they did not truly believe it was possible. One man believed- he practiced and practiced. He was able to do the before though of physically impossible and run the mile in under 4 minutes!!!!! His record stood for only 46 days before it was broken. Once others knew it was possible they to were able to do it.

If you truly believe- you can make anything happen. It won't be easy, you may try and fail but if you keep going after your goal- YOU CAN DO IT.

YOU HAVE TO FEEL IT, TOUCH IT, BREATH IT AND ABOVE ALL BELIEVE IT!!!!!

Teresa Cloninger

I always go into every sales call with a positive attitude! I keep the frame of mind that I'm going to close every sale! Being confident and determined to come out on top of every sales call are two of the most important sales tactics you can have. Go in with your head high and always remember, "What's the worst that could happen, they can't take your birthday away!"

David Bradley

Be your own self fulfilling prophecy! If you expect to succeed than you will. Set reachable goals that wont discourage you. At the same time will challenge you enough to keep you interested in reaching those goals.

Brian Spraggins

2. Why should you spend time reviewing your success?

A class of high school basketball players with similar skills were divided into three groups to conduct an experiment.

Group one was told not to practice shooting free throws for one month.

Group two was told to practice shooting free throws an hour a day for a month.

Group three was told to practice shooting free throws an hour a day for a month - but only in their imaginations.

At the end of the month, all three groups were tested. The group that didn't practice slipped slightly in its percentage of free throw successes. The group that practiced an hour a day stayed the same. But the third group, which practiced only in their minds, increased their success rate by two percentage points. How could actual practice, such as that done by the second group, fail to improve performances as much as practicing in the mind? The explanation is that in your mind, you never miss a shot.

What if... you did the same thing the basket ball players did with the sales calls you have lined up for tomorrow?

What if... you took 3 minutes before turning in for the night and pictured each prospect welcoming you with open arms?

What if... you mentally reviewed everything you did RIGHT during the day rather than the mistakes you inevitably made?

Would it make a difference? You bet it would!

Several years ago I was asked to do some sales training for a company that sold food plans. The first thing I did was go through their complete sales training program to see what they were teaching. Everything seemed perfect except for one thing.

Everyone in the training class was told over and over again they should expect to expect to make two sales per week. Here's what I did. I had the next class of trainees told that they should expect to make 4 sales per week. All other aspects of the training were identical for both classes.

After their first month in the field, the second group had outsold the first group by a ratio of nearly two to one. Were they luckier? Was the second group getting all the breaks while the first group was having a run of bad luck?

No. The second class saw in their mind making four sales a week.

Corporations study their most profitable products. Profits permit companies to grow, in much the same way your successes challenge you to grow. The companies that grow the most have focused and improved on what they have done successfully. Did they do it by concentrating on their least profitable products or services? Do they constantly review their mistakes over and over again? No.

They increase their profits by concentrating on the products and services producing the most profit.

What does this mean to your selling success?

It means that your opportunities can be limitless, if you concentrate on your success rather than your mistakes. That doesn't mean you stop making mistakes. It means you change your attitude toward mistakes.

Instead of saying "If only I had done it this way or said something different," you view the mistake for what it is, something that didn't work. The key is to become well acquainted with your successes. What you are looking for are the things you are doing right.

Successful companies spend HUGE amounts of money each year in advertising to proclaim the merits of their products and services. You hold the key to your own selling success, and it can only be found in your individual performance. These nuggets are like the successful products and services the corporations concentrate on to produce the most profit.

Let's look at it from another perspective. Suppose you know two different people. One seems to fail at whatever they attempt. The other is very successful and does exceptionally well in your specific area of sales. Whose experience should you study to benefit most: the repeated failure, or the success? Whose secret would you rather know?

Successful sales people make plenty of mistakes; however they relive and build on their achievements and successes resulting in higher and higher expectations. You will never be free of mistakes nor can you become successful by simply trying to avoid mistakes. You will continue to have many successes and many failures.

If corporations can increase their profits by identifying their greatest "pay-off" products and services, you can increase your sales by reliving your successful sales calls.

At the end of every sales call you have a choice. You can be upset or discouraged by your mistakes or you can be excited and proud of the things you did right. Even if you did not make the sale you still did several things right. By reviewing your successes you strengthen them and give a better performance on your next call.

Try this: At you next sales meeting have 4 or 5 sales people describe their most successful sales call.

What is the toughest job you have to do on a daily basis? What is the one thing that keeps you from making sales, keeps you worrying about business, and keeps you feeling insecure?

I am going to identify it but first, let me assure you, we are all effected by it. Regardless of how long you have been in sales or how many setback you have to face. Not only in your sales activities, but also in other areas of your life.

Here it is, the hardest thing we have to do. We have to see in our mind not the way things are, but the way things can become.

This is easy to do when things are going along smooth. When customers are buying, progress is being made and things are looking pretty good. When we are in the "success frame of mind" it is easy to see all the possibilities. However, when we are up against some tough times, that is when we are tested. That is when we really find out how difficult it is to see things the way we want them to become. Especially when we look around and we are in a seemingly impossible situation.

The law of nature insists that we grow. When we are growing and improving we are naturally positive and excited about what we are doing. However, when we run into an obstacle and we go backwards, just the opposite takes place in how we feel. All of a sudden we see ourselves filled with apprehension and failure.

I was watching a TV show a few days ago on the Hallmark channel. Now, I'm a guy and the Hallmark channel is by no means my first choice of channels to watch. But I am also married so certain sacrifices have to be made. Anyway, during the story this little girl kept having dreams about monsters. She went to the "good witch" for some help. The "good witch" told the little girl NOT to think about bunny rabbits before she went to sleep. So the little girl went to sleep saying over and over again "don't think about bunny rabbits, don't think about bunny rabbits!" Well you know the rest of the story.

What does this stupid little story have to do with selling?

Here it is: "Don't think about how FANTASTIC you are going to feel when you make the sale. Don't think about how you are going to feel when you land the new account! Don't think about how your self esteem is going to shoot through the roof when you are standing in front of the sales team telling them how you turned everything around and your sales are on fire!"

We eventually become what we think about. So promise me this, you won't think about success. Promise me you won't think about how you are going to prosper. Instead do this: think about monsters. Think about how everyone else is in a rut so you should be too.

Anyway, I think I will go to the bookstore and see what they have on witchcraft! Whatever it takes to sell, right?

I believe that the most important thing in life, be it your career or your personal relationships is to just keep trying. If you do something wrong. In either relationship the only thing you can do is to learn from it and try not to do that particular thing in the same way again. If you just don't give up you're bound to succeed sooner or later. The Only "bad mistake" is the one you don't learn from

Brian Spraggins

I believe that every one should review their success by looking both at the good and the bad. Every one knows that you will not get every customer now no matter what you say or do. You're going to have good days and bad days. You will have some customers knocking down the doors for your products and others that will turn you down no matter what you say or do. What seems like a good sale pitch to one customer might bomb with the next. Each prospect must be approached differently. Don't let yourself get discouraged over a lost sale. Go on to the next one and do it over and over until you achieve your goals. Reviewing yourself daily will help build positive attitude and strengthen your performance for the next time.

Laura Arnett

I review success in steps: Getting in the door is a success. Seeing someone and being able to talk to them and ask them questions is a success. Success grows with each step you make. You may not always have success the first time around, but if at first you don't succeed try, try again.

Kathie Luttrell

It is important to review your success because it makes you realize how well you are doing and makes you want to do better and strive for more. If you focus on the mistakes you've made it will never motivate you to be more and do more therefore ignoring your successes.

Morgan Clarke

3. What is a simple method for setting goals?

Would you like to be more successful? Would you like to make more money? Would you like to take more exciting vacations? Would you like to have more security for you and your family? You can have everything you ever wanted. All you have to do is one thing.

What is the one thing it takes to be successful? In order to evaluate this question it is first necessary to understand what "success" is and what all successful people have in common. It is probably safe to assume that you want to be more successful.

By definition, success is the realization of a worthy goal. Success is different for every individual. For some people, an annual income of $25,000 would be a success, for another it may be $225,000. Whatever it may be for you, there are specific characteristics that you must have in common with other successful people in order to achieve true success.

A goal is the one thing - the single most important factor in achieving success. Without a realistic goal, you will never know when you have reached your success level.

The goal must be realistic, measurable and obtainable. As time passes, your goal can always be adjusted upward. However, if your initial goal is to be worth $1,000,000 by the year end and you are currently only worth $100,000 with an annual income of $50,000 a year and this is November, you most likely will never be able to reach it and therefore, it is unrealistic.

Biting off a job in small portions makes the eventual achievement of the total task seem easier and manageable. That is why a 90-day goal is so effective. Successful people set a goal, re-evaluate their goal, and scale it upward toward an even greater accomplishment.

So many people never get anywhere in their lives because they don't know where they are trying to go. If you don't have a destination you will have no reason to make plans? If you don't know where you are going, you won't be able to help anyone else reach their destination?

Several years ago there was a study done at Harvard University. The graduating class was polled and it was found that only 3 percent of the class had any clear goals set for their future. Twenty years later, the researchers followed up on that same graduating class. The 3 percent who had clearly defined goals accomplished more and made more money than the other 97 percent combined!

Once you get into a habit of goal-setting, you will wonder how you ever managed to accomplish anything before.

The best goal is a 90-day SMART goal. The SMART system works - it has stood the test of time. SMART is shorthand for the five characteristics of a well-designed goal.

S = specific. When a goals is specific, it tells you exactly what you have to do, when, and how much. Because the goal is specific, you can easily measure your progress. A 90-day sales objective is specific.

M = measurable. What good is a goal that you can't measure? If your goal is not measurable, you never know whether you are making progress toward successful completion. A 90-day sales objective is measurable.

A = attainable. A goal must be realistic and attainable. The best goal is one that requires you to stretch a bit to achieve it. That is, the goal is neither out of reach nor below standard performance. If a goal is set too high or too low it become meaningless. A 90-day sales objective is attainable.

R = relevant. Eighty percent of productivity comes from only 20 percent of your activities. Relevant goals address the 20 percent. A 90-day sale goal will give you a long list of benefits when it is achieved.

T = time limit. A goal must have starting point, ending point, and fixed duration. Commitment to a deadline helps to focus your efforts on completion of the goal on or before the due date. A goal without a deadline for completion tends to be overtaken by the day-to-day crises that invariably arise. A 90-day sales goal has a very clear time limit.

What about long range goals?

A five year sales goal is much more attainable if it is worked on 90-days at a time. Set your long range goals - but break them down into 90-day increments.

Sometimes I set goals, then assume the path to reach the goal will require suffering and sacrifice – which is a recipe for failure. A better idea would be to set a goal and pay attention to the effect it has on my present reality. I need to set goals that yield a positive effect on my life whenever I think about them, long before the final outcome is actually achieved.

Treat goal-setting as a way to enhance your present reality, not as a way to control the future.

Gary Caudill

How to lose your best sales preson.

I came off of a very good year of $650,0000 in new business, only to find that management set my goals for the next year to be 1,000,000 in new business.

"Out of all the sales people we know you can do it!"

Hello! If I could acheive something like that I would be considered a super hero! Then management felt they needed to help me reach the goal. They added a'punishment factor!' My commission would be cut by the % I missed achieving my goal (reviewed monthly). 1st month down to 97% lost 3%, by May I was down to 88% losing 12% of my commission, and by July I told them to stick it! I was gone.

David Vize

Employers can tend to be stingy with compliments and pats on the back. So how do you know if you are satisfying or exceeding their requirements and expectations? Many times you only find out when you are not. So an employer-set goal has the advantage of letting you know where you stand with them.

A personal goal lets you know where you stand with yourself. Have you really done all that you know you are capable of doing or do you need to come up with some more effort?

Crocker Smith

I once read that, "the road of someday leads to nowhere."

It never ceases to amaze me how people just coast along in life Hoping to reach goals they never set. People spend more time shopping for the next big bargin in the weekend flyers and looking for new cars then they do investing into their future goals and dreams. I can remember the first time I actually set a goal and achieved it. I think I was more inspired by the fact that I actually did what I set out to do then the financial reward I received from it. Knowing I did something that all my friends and family said was impossible especially with my skill set. Boy! Am I glad I don't listen very well! The reason you are were you are this point in time is because of your actions,behaviors,attitudes and beliefs. If you want more out of life then you need to become more personally and you need to write out your goals and review them on a daily basis.

Dwayne Mitchell

My comment on this lesson may not be popular but this is what I have found to be true. As a manager I am big on goal setting, however, I learned early on that a sure fire way to destroy moral is to set unattainable goals. Yes, goals can be lofty, but not unrealistic. There truly are only so many ours in a work day. No one wants you to create burnout in their employees. It is a thin line.

Lynn Mosely

4. What are your points of difference?

It's true! You can't sell anybody anything, you can't change people's minds, you can't persuade them to do something against their will and you can't get people to buy based on price alone.

We have to be crystal clear about what our job really is. We think that we have to apply pressure, use special psychological techniques and force people to buy from us.

Regardless of whether you are a supervisor, a sales person, a waitress, a service provider or a marketing manager your job is the same: Your job is to help people make good decisions - and the more informed you are about your products and services, the more valuable you are to your customer.

You can make your life a whole lot easier starting right now by stop thinking that you have to be clever and use some secret selling technique to get people to buy from you. All you have to do is answer this question; Why should I buy from you? When someone asks that question of you what they are really asking is "I need help making a good decision!"

You might sell the exact same thing as everyone else, but you point out the differences of why your product or service is unique to their business. Sure everyone else is selling the same thing; however, what makes yours different is you have asked your clients about what they want from the product. You have listened and taken notes and figured out what your customer is trying to accomplish. You then give the customer the solution to their problem. The best part is, it has not cost you anything because you are not charging extra, just helping the customer make a good decision. You are adding value.

The "point of difference" of your product is the extra service you offer. This extra, in a sense, is your consulting service. And as a customer, when I can get free consulting service with a product or service the decision of who to buy from is easy. Even if it is a meal in a restaurant.

The secret of persuading people is that there is no secret. Just call on enough people and show them why doing business with you is the best decision they can possibly make! And if everything is equal, the deciding factor will be the fact that YOU go with the deal.

How am I supposed to learn everything about the products I sell when there is so much confusing information that I have to muddle through?

The answer - points of difference.

To increase your product knowledge, compare points of difference in the products. Each point of difference can be viewed as positive or negative depending on what your customer is looking for. Each point will change the price and the value of the product.

Considering the number of line items it takes to maintain a competitive inventory, gaining sufficient product knowledge is a long, slow process. With new products and programs being introduced continuously and old ones being changed or discontinued, it becomes a real challenge to stay on top of the necessary information.

The secret of gaining product knowledge is to compare points of difference. What is the difference between the new and the old? What is the difference between your product and a competitor's product? Each point of difference will change the price and the value of the product.

As a professional sales person you must be able to sell value added products. What kind of definition would you come up with when you are asked the meaning of "Value Added Selling"?

The best answer is to know the points of difference and sell your differences as a benefit.

A sales person who can answer objections with good solid facts and product information will out perform the person who "wings it" every time.

To gain the respect of your customers and earn their business, product knowledge should be a daily activity.

To increase product knowledge continually ask questions that help customers make the right choices. Read the trade journals and clip articles that contain helpful information for your customers.

All product knowledge has to be translated into customer benefits if it is to be of value to the customer. When selling, it does little good to focus on the features of the products or services offered. It makes little difference how long your company has been in business, how large your facility is, or how many employees you have unless it can be used to solve your customers problems.

Here is how you might use this to raise the bar on your own services. Take out any one of your software boxes, or stop in the computer store and browse through the software department. Notice how they are always comparing the old version with the new upgraded version. What would an upgraded version of YOU look like? What points of difference would there be between the old you and the you that you will become with just a slight nudge?

Here are a few examples:

The old version of you compared to the new version of you

OLD - Ho-hum about what I do

NEW - Really excited about my profession

OLD - Take care of my customers

NEW - Give extraordinary customer service

OLD - Only put in enough effort to get buy

NEW - Always go the extra mile for every customer

OLD - Customers know I appreciate them

NEW - Go out of my way to say thanks and show appreciation for my customers

When selling yourself and your services you must be able to convince your prospective customer that you are the right choice, you must know your strengths and be sure you transmit them so the message is received. Your customers can buy products from anyone. In an industry where everyone is selling the same products the most important point of difference is you. YOU are the customer's link to the universe. YOU are the one thing that really makes a difference. This puts a responsiblity on you to be resourse - a problem solver. A typical sales person focuses on price while a true consultant finds out from the customer what he or she wants and helps them get it.

Ask yourself this question. How much could I get someone to pay me to listen to my sales pitch? Most likely the answer is zero. However, consultants get paid thousands of dollars an hour to do what? Ask questions.

Here is an interesting fact I just received from my publisher. 85% of all books are purchased by women, and 95% of all books are never read past the first chapter. That means that if you simply put in a little effort and spend time reading and studying you will be amazed at the immediate difference.

I think this goes back to the difference between a salesman and a consultant. I tell my prospects, especially the price driven ones that I can't save them to being millionaires. On the other hand I can help them build their businesses so that they can be millionaires.

I tell them that the difference between them and Wendy's is that they serve better food than Wendy's and that Wendy's hires people to get the job done right the first time so that it is consistent and focuses instead on growing their market share.

I tell them that Wendy's could save a ton of money by buying their product on sale at the grocery store.

Then I ask the customer why they don't run their operation like a big chain. Serve outstanding food, consistently day in and day out at a competitive price and market the hell out of it. Hire the people that will help them do that effectively with the companies that are committed to that growth and they cannot and will not lose.

Then I ask them when their current rep gave them a menu idea or told them something that put money in their pocket.

Dave Ferren

Over the past 2 years I have learned so much on the differences in products. I'm learning why there are different case prices whether it is quality, pack sizes or a brand name over an off brand. I have learned that if I didn't know the answer I would call someone and get the answer the customer wants to know. This has improved my sales and the customers confidence in me.

Scott Forgie

Product knowledge and customer knowledge go hand in hand. It is important to have product knowledge and how it can benefit your customer. If a customer asks me about a product that I am not familiar with I can call one of our buyers and usually get the information requested on the spot. I can usually have a sample in the customer's hand by the next day. I am the "point of difference" to my customers by service that my competitor's cannot or will not deliver.

Phil Hackett

In order to know your "points of difference" between your product and your competitor's, you not only need to have good product knowledge of your own merchandise. You must also be very familiar with the competitor's products. Never miss an opportunity to learn something new.

Larry Edmondson

I represent a family owned independent in a market where 3 "big box" distributors are located within 10 miles of each other, and another one is only 40 miles away. Having a combined 20 years with two of them in the past, I get very enthusiastic giving the "points of difference" in my company and formatting it in a "features and benefits" way with real emphasis on the "benefits" of doing business with us.

Doug Barringer

The "extra service" you offer your client or prospect is your point of difference. YOU are the added value. To achieve this you must be extremely knowledgeable about your product, and stay on top of the continually changing market. You also have to use you "differences" as a benefit, a positive thing, ultimately "I" am the person who can make the difference in my customer's eyes.

Brooke Knight

Product knowledge is very important in the world of a salesman or saleswoman. The more youi know and learn about the product or service you're selling, the better off you are going to be. Everyone you attempt to sell to is going to have questions and you want to be able to answer them without fumbling around looking for the right answer. You want to know and be able to respond with the answer right away. Another important thing to remember is that if you don't know the answer, don't pretend that you do. Let them know that your not sure but you will be happy to find out and let them know. You don't want to be known as the salesperson who tells people what they want to hear, not what they need to know!

David Bradley

Product knowledge in my opinion is very important however I do not like to put all the emphasis on the product knowledge. Put emphasis on being a people person and someone that people want to meet and talk with and then you will be able to share your product knowledge. And if you don't know the answer they already like you enough to let you find it out. The product information is somewhere for you to obtain. How many times have you asked a friend about something and they didn't know but they said they would definitely find out for you and you got mad, you haven't. So be a people person and a friendly person and they will work with you however you want them to.

Derek Yelton

5. Do you have a sense of urgency?

This whole thing with the economy has proven ONE THING. The customer is KING. All those people who think that companies are in business to make something, produce something, deliver something, or fix something are finding out that if no one buys their products or services they are history. And in my mind, that is a good thing. When anyone in the company thinks that taking care of a customer is someone else's job, well, the handwriting is on the wall.

Our economy is a SALES DRIVEN ECONOMY, PERIOD. You and I, and every other person who spends a dollar on anything has proven that. If we don't get the customer service we expect, we are gone to a competitor in a New York minute. (For those of you who are reading this from New Zealand, Australia or Canada, a New York minute is 45 seconds!)

And since we are ALL selling something, it is more important that YOU keep the edge on YOUR own service that you provide. Your competitors are hungry and they are after YOUR business. And in some cases, they are successful in taking away a customer. I want to challenge you to do ONE thing today that will make a huge difference in how your business grows. I want you to commit to using the UPOD strategy.

Have you ever heard of the acronym UPOD? If not you are in for one of the most impressive selling strategies you will ever use.

But first, let me ask you a couple of questions. How you answer will help you examine yourself and see if have the internal drive that will help you take full advantage of the UPOD strategy.

Are you hungry? Do you want more? To succeed in sales you MUST be hungry and have a strong desire for success.

The key question to ask yourself: "What motivates me to keep doing the things that are necessary for success?"

Am I a goal setter, do I have personal and financial goals big enough to make me do the things the failures do not like to do?

There are many sales people who are content to pick up the small orders without any desire for a bigger piece of the pie. You must be the type of sales person who looks for the opportunity to polish your skills every day. By giving your best performance on every call and always asking yourself how you could have done better - you can be classified as a true professional.

I am used to dealing with professionals. I can tell a professional before I even meet them in person. They have a single quality that shows up in everything they do.

And when you deal with someone who is NOT a professional, you sure can tell the difference. Do you have this quality? Can you guess what it is?

Here is an example of what this single quality is NOT!

I am selling two of my properties. I am not using a real estate broker, simply because the folks who are buying the properties are currently living in them. I have contacted the mortgage broker to arrange for the financing, the closing company to handle the paperwork, and you would think the rest would be simple. All you need is 4 or 5 documents to go along with the application. Well, it is like pulling teeth to get those documents. All kinds of delays. Every excuse you can think of. I have spent more time chasing around to get things done than you can imagine. After three weeks it STILL isn't done. It should have taken one day at the most!

Now let me give you another example.

A client of mine called and wanted to set up a series of three seminars for their customers. Within 5 minutes Ray and I had all the details worked out. Within 24 hours Ray had the locations, the times, the initial promotional piece, lunch arrangements for our participants, and the announcement out to his sales team. THAT is what you call a "sense of urgency!" THAT is what you call being a professional. THAT is why they are a leading distributor in

43

the Midwest. THAT IS THE SINGLE QUALITY (Thanks Ray!)

As a professional you always have the feeling that there are things that need to be done. Not from pressure or stress, but because you WANT to get them done. They are on your TO DO list and are there for a reason. You are motivated by end results and keep your eyes on the big picture, the overall plan and objectives.

Do you call your customers when there is a potential problem? For example, if a product is short on their order do you call your customer in advance and let them know, or do you let it go by and hope they have enough left in stock to get them by?

When you hear a piece of news that could possibly effect one of your customers do you make it a special point to let them know, or do you assume they will get the information themselves?

When one of your customers has a problem and calls you for help, do you drop everything and do "whatever it takes" to help with the solution, or do you hesitate and hope that by the time you return the call the problem will go away?

That is the true mark of a professional. That is the single quality: A sense of urgency!

A sense of urgency is a skill that can be developed with practice. By adopting an attitude of "do it now" you can solve many small problems before they turn in a lost sale or a lost customer. By taking care of things immediately you impress your customers more than you can imagine.

Small things like returning phone calls within minutes rather than hours, dropping thank you cards in the mail the same day rather than two or three days later (if at all), make a big difference.

Now for the UPOD. A while ago I used this with an editor I was working with. He was much more impressed with my use of the UPOD strategy than if I had done things the normal way. UPOD stands for Under Promise Over Deliver. I received an email and was asked if I had any more articles. I told him it would take a couple of days. I then kicked in the UPOD (I have used this so often it has become a habit). I sent him an article within ten minutes. Here's the editor's response "That was the fastest couple of days in history."

Try it the next time a customer calls and asks for something. Give them a longer period of time and then kick in your "sense of urgency," your "whatever it takes," your "desire for success" attitude, and watch the response you get!

One of my customers called me very late and wanted extra cases of a special order item that they knew they were getting in a couple of days. They had a request to cater a party and badly needed the business. I told the owner, "I'll do my best, but due to the short notice, I can't guarantee it." Knowing how good our buyers are and how quick they are to respond to our needs, after that phone call I felt pretty sure the request would be successful. I personally delivered the special request, they were absolutely in awe, and it further solidified our professional relationship. UPOD is a game changer!

Stephen Carney

The more you accomplish now is less you have to worry about later. The same goes with how you respond to your customer issues and problems. If you take care of it quickly you reduce the chance of these things adding up. The more problems you put off will cause a lot more stress on a person and cause them to loose focus on there goals. I have a sense of urgency in regards to everything I do. The military has taught to me to be light on my feet and to adapt and overcome and it has stuck with me throughout.

Jason Kirouac

One of my past company's strongest advocates had a machine vandalized on a Saturday and called me saying it had to be running by Monday morning. The parts were 5 days away. We cannibalized a new machine on our yard for the parts and had his machine up and running Sunday afternoon.

For the next 8 years he has told many, many people about our exceptional service and this really helped increase our sales. It was almost like having another salesman who worked for free but better.

Crocker Smith

In order to become successful, you must a sense of urgency and a "whatever it takes" attitude when it comes to handling issues or concerns with a customer. I believe that I get a very positive response from contacts when I meet them initially and follow up with an e-mail or note immediately. I am still fresh on their mind, and they see that I am dedicated to helping them SUCCEED. This gives the client the feeling that you want their business, and it doesn't seem like you are BEGGING them either. It's the little things that make ALL the difference.

Brooke Knight

Some say that I have too much of a sense of urgency, but I have found that customers do appreciate a quick response. I have discovered that you can add on to an under promise, but it is hard to take away if you promise too much.

Jordan de la Morandiere

I have heard of the UPOD acronym a couple of years ago. I used to fall into the category of OPUD (Over Promise Under Deliver).. which isn't a good place to be! I learned the hard way, to reverse that way of thinking. Sure you want to impress your customers, and yes you do understand their sense of urgency regarding the situation - but it's best to promise a for sure solution instead of trying to pull a rabbit out of a hat. I have also found, that I give them a back up solution. So they know if solution A doesn't happen - here's solution B that will kick in. The end result is that the customer is satisfied since they know that you took their urgent situation seriously, and you are trying to ensure that their needs are being met.

Joanne Welch

6. How do you make people care about you?

Sometimes you have to take a negative approach to get a positive response, sometimes you have to be creative to get someone's attention in the first place, and sometimes you have to really think outside the box to make people take notice.

I am going to give you an example that is going to blow your mind. But first, let me show you a couple of things I have in my files that really seem to work, and some that don't.

Whenever I am on an airplane or in a crowd of strangers I am asked what I do. According to the experts you should have an "elevator speech" for these occasions. You should be able to tell people what you do by the time the elevator makes it from one floor to the next.

I designed a clever 30 second speech and it really seemed to turn people off. As soon as I said I was a "sales trainer" I could see the expression on their face turn to panic. They immediately said they don't use sales trainers, or they have a company employee who does their sales training. They had a ready made objection. So by following the advice of the experts, I was turning people off in less than 30 seconds.

Back to the drawing board. I took a different approach by thinking outside the box.

I created a "shock" effect and I am now able to get people's interest and have some fun at the same time. Now, when they ask me what I do, here is what I say:

"I show people how to stay 4 steps ahead of the sheriff, would you like to know what those 4 steps are?" And they always say YES?

I give them four quick steps that would be applicable to them and ask which step would be most helpful. If they say "step 3" I give them a really good sound bite of information on step 3. I then get their business card and follow up with some more helpful information.

I am getting ready to do a 5,000 piece mailing and guess what will be on the envelope? You got it: "How to stay 4 steps ahead of the sheriff, would you like to know what the 4 steps are?"

When you are approaching a new account think of your first few words as the sales copy on the envelope. The job of the sales copy is NOT to make the sale, but to get them OPEN UP!

By the way, click here for a pdf file with my 4 steps. This is what's going to be inside the envelope. Keep in mind that if they don't open the envelope the sale will NEVER be made! The same with your opening line. If you don't hit the right button the door doesn't open.

Here are some of the standard openers and my translation. If you are guilty you might spend a little time creating something that works for you. Be easy on yourself, everyone has used them.

"I am sorry for interrupting."

Translation: I really don't amount to much - you are much more important than I am - you see I am just a doormat waiting for someone to wipe their feet on me.

"I know you are busy."

Translation: I really don't have any respect for you or your time - you are a busy and important person and I am intruding in you day.

"I was in the neighborhood."

Translation: I am not very organized - I simply drift through my day from neighborhood to neighborhood making random calls on people and waste their time.

"Do you need anything?"

Translation. I am really not much of a sales person and I was wondering if there are any crumbs left over from a real sales person who has been here.

"I wanted to stop by and introduce myself."

Translation. I am really not ambitious enough to have done some homework about you so I guess I will tell you about ME.

I think you get the point. Things are different out there today, so you have to be different or they eat you alive.

Today's customers are being bombarded with an estimated 3,000 sales and marketing messages every day. How do you stand out and set yourself apart from the crowd? You have to hit them with a HUGE BENEFIT. A benefit that will have the same power as if you hit them between the eyes with a baseball bat!

How should you make your entrance into an account?

First: Attitude. You should always assume an attitude of confidence and purpose. Never apologize for making the call. Never feel like you are interrupting. Never say, "I was in the neighborhood" as if your call was not important. Never say, "I wanted to stop by and introduce myself." Who cares?

There is a psychological law that makes the prospect react and respond to the attitude and action expressed by you the sales person. There is nothing complicated about it, except the results that come when you put this psychological law into effect. Make the call with confidence.

Second. A huge SPECIFIC BENEFIT. For example.: "I am here to show you how you can lower your operating expenses by $5,323 dollars per quarter -or- I am here to show you how increase your invoice size by 25 cents, which equates to $813 per week, let me show you how I figured it based on your current volume -or- I have a product that will cut your cleaning time by 23% resulting in a labor cost savings of $103 per week or $5,356 per year."

I can hear you now. "But Bob, I have to call on my accounts every week!" How could I possibly come up with a new money saving or money making idea for my customers EVERY WEEK?"

My answer. How many line items do you have? 2,000? 4,000? 8,000? 10,000? Every line item you have in your inventory represents an opportunity. How many services do you have? 27? 37? 47? Or how about 57?

I can still hear you. "But Bob, all my competitors are selling on price and I have to meet their prices or lose the business."

What if your competitor was giving their product away FREE? What if there was very little quality difference between your product and the "free" product? What if their method of distribution was much more efficient than yours? Could you sell against that kind of competition? No?

Well someone was given a sales challenge to sell against that kind of market condition. And they are very successful. The product is bottled water. How do they do it? Do they lower their price and try to compete with tap water? Do they badmouth the water company and tell their customers "yea, it may be free, but look at what you get!"

Is bottled water really any better? I gave it the ultimate taste test. I put two bowls of water in front of my dog – one from a bottle that I paid over a dollar for – the other from the sink faucet. My dog tried both of them. Which one do you think she preferred? The tap water! Did I switch to tap water? No. I still pay an outrageous price for a bottle of water.

Why? Somehow the perceived value of water in a bottle is a strong enough benefit for me to fork over my hard earned cash.

Every item in your warehouse has within it a huge benefit to the customer or it wouldn't be in the warehouse. All you have to do is find ONE BENEFIT PER WEEK and present it to all your customers.

Lets do the math. Thirty-five accounts x one benefit per week x 52 weeks = 1,820 benefit presentations per year.

Even a blind hog can find an acorn once in a while. If you make ONE THOUSAND EIGHT HUNDRED AND TWENTY benefit presentations per year – you will sell something – even if by accident.

The bottom line. You walk into your account. There have been 2,999 people trying to sell this person today and you are number 3,000.

Do you say – "I'm sorry for interrupting?"

Do you say – "I know you are busy?"

Do you say – "I was in the neighborhood?"

Do you say – "Do you need anything?"

Do you say – "I wanted to stop by and introduce myself?"

Only if you want the customer to say – "Who cares?"

Benjamin Franklin drives home the point when he said: "Make yourselves sheep and the wolves will eat you."

I like the idea of presenting a bold idea to a prospect on the first call. I am going to sit down today and come up with a list of ideas on how to gain attention of my prospects on the first call. I don't want the person I am calling on to forget me as soon as I leave, I want to make a lasting impression.

Jim Chill

The most difficult part of the equation is me, the sales rep. I love the prop idea. Though I can't "vent" I can have some sort of hand out that, when given at the appropriate time, will help me tell my story. This works particularly well early on when you are not quite secure in your own skin. The key is to practice your opening at home. Write it out and give it to the mirror, your dog(biscuits work really well on them and will build your confidence-they can't resist) and your wife. The more you do it the better you will be. The thing to remember is that in a cold call situation your goal is to get permission to come back.

James Ruth

There is usually never a "good" time when calling on a potential customer for the first time...second...or third time. You suggest our approach should be specific and we should have done our homework before we make our grand entrance. However, sometimes we may not have been able to obtain a lot of information about that account that will allow us to be as specific as you state.

It is that first conversation with the potential customer that usually paints the whole picture or at least most of it. In my short term experiences, so far, I have found that it is easy to get the first conversation; it's the second one that seems a little tougher to come by. The second meeting is the one when you have to really put it out there and tell them what you have to offer and be specific in what you can do for them.

Liz Vaughan

I have finally come up with an introduction that I love. I like to ask "did I catch you at a bad time?". The contact person is programmed to answer "NO". This shows the prospective clients that you care about their time and don't want to be too pushy. I think they appreciate the fact that you know they have schedules and deadlines to meet too. It's just another way I look to differentiate myself and the company I represent.

Becky Akins

I loved this lesson. I have been guilty of saying, "let me introduce myself" and I feel this lesson demonstrates how that can backfire on my ability to get to know my prospect. One thing I would like to say is that, the reason I buy bottled water, in not for the taste of it. There is a benefit to drinking it. We all should probably drink more water and having it at our finger tips to take on the run allows us to do something good for ourselves in the mist of a very busy day. If you point out to your prospects how you my benefit them in a busy day, you cant go wrong. The prospect will not want to do business with you because you are just like all the other companies, but because you bring something to the table to make their day easier.

Tonya Sauer

I especially love this lesson because reemphasizes that we should not apologize for doing our job. We are very busy as well. I get especially irritated when people miss our pre scheduled appointment because it says that their time is somehow more important than mine. I am not a big fan of the 'drop in' appointment because I feel it is an imposition of someone's time. It's different than an information gathering cold call. You need to always present yourself like an organized BUSY, respectful business person.

Marquesa Ortega

This is a great lesson. So many times we all have walked in and said I just wanted to come by and introduce myself. In theory it sounds good and I have done it more times than I would like to admit. It makes sense that we shouldn't do this. We should go into a company and show them who we are and what we do. We need to do our homework on them so we can be better prepared when we walk through the door. At that point we aren't "intruding" or "just stopping by". We are there with a purpose, we are there to be the resource that they need, even if they don't know it yet.

Brandon Sanchez

Sometimes I feel as if most of my cold call customers are graduates of the 'How To Defeat A Sales Person Before They Get Past The First Sentence" correspondence course. A few of them have actually started walking backwards after I introduce myself. The winner was when I asked the General Manager of a mid-size company if I could have his card and he said "No!".

You can't force someone to listen to you or buy from you so you have to learn a different way to get your message across without aggravating them. And everyone is different so it takes a lot of ingenuity.

Crocker Smith

7. Do you feel insecure and worried about sales?

Let's go back to Colonel Sander for a minute. As you remember Colonel Sanders owned a restaurant that seated 142 people in Corbin, Kentucky, where he perfected his secret blend of 11 herbs and spices and the basic cooking technique that is still used today.

In 1950 a new interstate highway was planned to bypass the town of Corbin. Seeing an end to his business, the Colonel closed his restaurant and auctioned off his equipment. After paying his bills he was broke at the age of 65. He was reduced to living on his $105 Social Security checks.

Confident of the quality of his fried chicken, the Colonel devoted himself to the chicken franchising business that he started in 1952. He traveled across the country by car visiting thousands of restaurants, cooking batches of chicken for the owners and their employees. If the reaction was favorable, he entered into a handshake agreement on a deal that stipulated a payment to him of a nickel for each chicken the restaurant sold.

By 1964, Colonel Sanders had 600 franchised outlets for his chicken in the United States and Canada. That year, he sold his interest in the company for $2 million to a group of investors. The Colonel remained a public spokesman for the company until he died in 1980. In 1976, an independent survey ranked the Colonel as the world's second most recognizable celebrity.

What does Colonel Sanders have to do with you?

Everything!

I don't care how good a sales person you are, it is unlikely that you will every sell more than 2 out of every 10 prospects on your first call. That is as certain as the sun coming up in the east every morning. It is just the way selling is.

It took Colonel Sanders 12 years to sell 600 people on his "nickel a chicken" concept. Let's do the math.

That is 50 sales per year, or one per week. To sell one per week he would have to make 5 presentations per week. Remember, that's the most anybody can sell on their first call - 20%. If you happen to have a run on sales and sell 30%, you will have a dry spell where you sell only 10%.

Five presentation per week is 250 per year. Over a 12 year period that is a whopping 3,000 presentations! I am sure that after he sold a certain number himself he hired someone to make the presentations. But still, it is one heck of an accomplishment!

And remember, he did this from age 65 to 77.

What do you think was going through his mind when 4 out of 5, or 8 out of 10 prospects turned him down. Knowing people the way I do, I'm sure some thought he was a joke, some told him to get lost, some told him he couldn't be serious. "A NICKLE A CHICKEN? WHERE DID YOU EVER COME UP WITH A CRAZY IDEA LIKE THAT?"

Do you think The Colonel felt insecure and worried about what he was trying to do? Do you think that when he was alone at night in his hotel in some strange town with his cooking equipment and spices, he had doubts about being able to get people to pay him as agreed?

I think you know the answer. And that brings us to you.

One of the hardest things to overcome is the feeling of insecurity when you are selling on commission for a living. Without the security of a guaranteed income your thoughts are continually interrupted by fears of failure, rejection and "what people will think if I don't make it."

This is serious for the person going through it. If you are on commission and only get paid when you make a sale, or in your own business and are totally responsible for earning an income, it is easy to have visions of not being able to pay your expenses. And sometimes you CAN'T pay your expenses and you have to deal with that as well.

The obvious solution most people will give you is to control your attitude - easy to say and does not really offer a solution. A positive attitude is the end result you are trying to achieve.

There are many short-term programs that give you a temporary relief such as "self talk", repeating affirmations and listening to motivation tapes. These activities are helpful, however, they are not dealing with the core of the problem.

The question is; how do you keep moving forward with a positive attitude when you feel insecure and unsure of yourself? This insecure feeling causes you to look into the future with apprehension no matter how hard you try to think positive. You still see negative results from the effort you are putting forth today.

You are not convinced that if you do the right things over and over again you will achieve the results you want. You can try affirmations by saying over and over to yourself, "I will make the sale", "I will get the new account" and still end up with negative results. Why? Because even as you say the words and visualize the results, you don't really expect it to happen! You don't get what you want, what you wish for, what you think about, what you visualize or what you affirm. You get what you expect.

Let's say you wanted to have a back up cash reserve of $25,000 in the bank. You could affirm to yourself "I have a bank account with $25,000 in it." You could write it down as a "written goal." You could think "positive" about it. And still – nothing happens.

Why? Because you really don't expect it to happen! You don't BELIEVE. You might feel good about it for a short time. But after a few weeks it will fade away. Reality will overtake you and you will file your $25,000 bank account idea away as a wish or a daydream or "it would be nice."

You have also reinforced the concept that affirmations, goal setting, positive thinking and visualization don't work. The next time you try to get something you want it becomes even more difficult because you not only have to overcome your current feelings of doubt and fear – you also have to deal with your past. "I've tried this before – it didn't work out – but I'll give it another shot". Then, no matter how hard you try, deep down inside you don't really expect it to happen and you are right - It doesn't.

You get what you expect. Nothing more - nothing less. If you want to increase your sales you have to really EXPECT IT TO HAPPEN.

There is only ONE THING that builds expectations – ACTION – doing something productive.

I think the secret Colonel Sanders used to overcome the feeling of insecurity that every human being feels was his DECISION TO KEEP GOING. Every morning he got up and presented his "nickel a chicken" concept to another restaurant. AND 4 OUT OF 5 TOLD HIM TO GET LOST!

There is a big lesson that Colonel Sanders taught us. The Colonel's secret to sales is action. Picking up the phone and making the call, asking for the order at the price you want, writing the letter, or sending a follow up card.

That is the secret spice of success - action. Doing it even when you would rather be tossed under a bus.

If a sales professional says that they never worry about sales they are telling a big fat lie. The bottom line is that we have to keep ourselves positive and motivated. I asked a client of mine what was the reason you chose to pay this higher mark up to do business with me. The answer was simple... he said that it was my attitude that helped him make the purchase. Before I enter an existing client or a potential client I make sure I have a clear head and project a positive attitude.

Becky Akins

Everyone feels insecure at some point in life. I still have days when I worry what's going to happen at the office today. Are we going to lose another client because the company itself is closing down? We have had several customers that we lost in the last 2 years because the customer is moving to another town. But we have to keep looking for new customers to replace the ones we have lost. It is not easy task to do everyday. Keeping a positive attitude is not always easy when you here "no we don't need your services," or when you have had meeting after meeting and you think things are going well and they still tell you no. But you must pick yourself up and carry on. Just like falling off your horse or bike, you must get up and keep trying.

Laura Arnett

The mind is a powerful thing and if you think it can happen than it can happen, if you think negative thoughts you will have negative actions. Although it's not easy to have a positive mind all the time it is the ongoing comments that either will help make you or break you. If you want something bad enough wouldn't you work hard enough to get it?

Jenn Snider

Wow! these past few lessons seem to be directed right at me. I am constantly worried about my sales, the competition. "You get what you expect" is a great line and almost an instant attitude adjustment.

Dominick Yarnal

Of course everyone worries about these things, but if you set back and worry about it instead of understanding it and facing it then you will be stuck worrying. Just focus on your job and what you have accomplished and move forward from the things you weren't as successful at.

Jamie R. Friend

I totally agree! You have to expect things to happen! You have to believe and have faith in yourself in order to make things happen for a prospect and for the company you work for. Every time you overcome obstacles, think of it as a learning experience that will make you a better sales person. You just need to believe in yourself and understand your job well enough in order to make things happen for any prospect!

Yessie Narvaez

I agree, you get what you expect and not simply what you wish for. It can be difficult to keep up the positive attitude, at all times. I try to remember that SOMETIMES I get things I didn't expect…sometimes I get better than what I expected!

Tonya Sauer

I think that most people in sales worry at some time about getting the sale or losing the sale. We have to be positive even when we are told no over and over again. If we don't believe in our service we can't sell that service. The company we are trying to sell to will see our hesitation and will automatically tune us out. When we want to get that big sale we need to be confident in not only the service but in ourselves as well, its not only the service they are buying but us as well.

Brandon Sanchez

Ahh…. Worry- in SMALL doses this is a very GOOD thing. In LARGE doses a very BAD thing; to much worry will become a self fulfilling prophesy. You KNOW you won't get the business? Your right- we inadvertently sabotage ourselves and WILL lose the business. But in small doses it galvanizes us to take the next steps, push a little harder and think outside of the box. The next thing you know- you have made the next call AND the one after that, went the extra mile and closed the business!!!!!

Worry is like Salt- a little goes a long way and improves the flavor- too much will ruin the pot!

Teresa Cloninger

I'm constantly worried about not being able to make a sale. I do, however, know that if I make enough sales calls, I'm going to make a sale. You have to know you have the ability and expect that you will make the sale. If you don't expect you're going to make the sale, what's the point of leaving your office to go see a potential client?

Matthew Thacker

The point is to be confidant. If you are worried, its going to show. You have to be positive and remember that these clients need you, they just don't know it yet. We have something great to offer, we just need the opportunity to share it.

Kimberly Burgess

I do my best not to worry about the next potential sale. In reality, we know as salespeople that not every sale we try to make is going to close in our favor. You have to learn to keep your head up and roll with the punches, because determination and persistence will eventually pay off and when it does it will make up for all those deals that didn't go through!

David Bradley

I always worry about sales, that's my nature, I worry about everything. But, I also think positive. My prior sales position was based strictly on commission. I think it is only human nature to worry about something you care about, you just have to maintain a balance so you don't appear to lack confidence.

Vickie Reihl

YES!!! I am always worried about sales. I am worried about not getting the sale, the competition taking it away, or if we don't find the RIGHT employee for them. This has already happened to me once. I feel that if I am not worried about it, then my heart and soul will not be put into my job. I am that type of person.

I believe 10 years from now I will still be worried about sales, but I am not worried about my ability to do my job!

Lisa Tharp

About the author Bob Oros

Regardless of whether you are reading one of his books or attending one of his programs, the most frequent comment is: "This guy has been there, he is one of us, I am going to use these strategies."

With over 2,000 speaking engagements in all 50 states and several international locations for manufacturers, distributors and associations, you can be sure you will get the results and information you are looking for. Prior to starting his speaking career, Bob served six years in the US Navy as a Communications Specialist and then worked his way from a street sales person to the position of National Sales Manager for a Fortune 200 company.

Bob has received awards for speaking, writing and marketing too numerous to mention.

Additional Topics by Bob Oros

Why Sales People Fail

The Key to Selling Anybody

Add Value to Every Product

Never Make the First Offer

How to Justify Your Price

Lost in 60 Seconds

One Good Reason to Buy

Control a Buyer's Attitude

How to Create Demand

Smoke Screen Objections

Take the Risk Out of Sales

How Small Companies Get Big